MAD®
LOBSTERS

AND OTHER ABOMINABLE HOUSEBROKEN CREATURES

WRITTEN & DRAWN BY
PAUL PETER PORGES

WARNER BOOKS

A Warner Communications Company

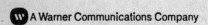

PAUL PETER PORGES:
Portrait of the Writer/Artist

by Nick Meglin,
Mad Magazine Editor

No one knows more about *"abominable creatures"* than *Paul Peter Porges,* who has been called an "abominable creature" all his life since his youthful days in the Vienna suburbs. He began his art career as a specialist for *Hugh's Hues,* a color company responsible for the exacting process of tinting the Blue Danube. As *"Azure Blue First Class,"* Porges quickly worked his way up through the ranks: *Cobalt Captain, Prussian Major, Cerulean Colonel,* and finally *Ultra-Marine Brigadier!* His *"Blue Period"* was followed by his *"Rosé Period"* when he painted the Red Sea, and later in England where he created his controversial *"Pink Floyd"* shade. Porges' colorful career hit rock-bottom soon afterwards in Yellowstone

National Park where he learned that he had been color blind all these years from an eye doctor while painting the Painted Desert. His *monumental* success thus invalidated, the artist lost his confidence and retreated to the Black Hills where he concentrated only on *blanc du blanc*, pen, brush, ink, and absurdity. His cartoons began appearing in major showcases, most notably the public restrooms in New York City's famed *"Gag Alley"* of Times Square. It was here that Porges' potential as an artist/writer was discovered. As a steady contributor for major magazines, it was only a matter of *Time* and *Newsweek* before *Mad* publisher William M. Gaines realized Porges was a natural for his magazine and paperback line.

It is said of true geniuses that *"they die, but their work lives on."* In the case of Paul Peter Porges, *he* lives on, but *his work* has been *dead* for years! See for yourself in this collector's edition of

MAD® LOBSTERS

AND OTHER ABOMINABLE HOUSEBROKEN CREATURES

TABLE OF CONTENTS

It's easy to like a lobster (especially with melted butter) but some of us find it difficult to drop the creature into boiling water. Well, there is an alternative! You can always serve a baloney sandwich instead and keep the lobster as a pet—just like a puppy or kitten. Of course, if you do keep this abominable creature as a pet, you'll want to teach it some ...

NIFTY TRICKS FOR HOUSEBROKEN LOBSTERS

START WITH SOME EASY TRICKS:

BEG!

8 ROLL OVER!

PLAY DEAD!

HOT BUTTER

RETRIEVE THE STICK!

9

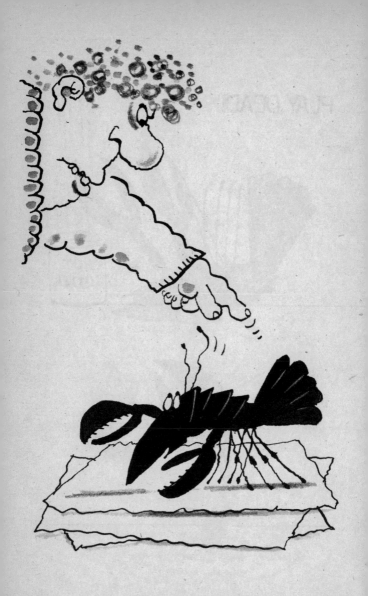

ON THE PAPER!

HEEL!

11

SHAKE CLAWS!

SLOWLY WORK UP TO SOME MORE DIFFICULT TRICKS:

TOSS THE BALL!

14   *GIVE A KISS!*

FETCH THE SNEAKER! 15

ATTACK!

SOON YOU'LL BE AMAZED AT WHAT YOU CAN TEACH YOUR LOBSTER:

19

21

AND IF HE DOESN'T PERFORM ALL THESE TRICKS:

BAD LOBSTER!

*L*obsters are not the only abominable pets in the world. Aquarium fish
rank right up there with lobsters. Why?
Because aquarium fish are so devious,
they trick us into thinking that all they
do is float around on the bottom of
their bowls all day! In fact, they actu-
ally frolic about when no one is watch-
ing! Like disgusting roaches in the
kitchen sink, they party and argue and
act weird like the rest of us! Join us
now as we listen in on some ...

FISHBOWL
CHATTER
EXPOSED

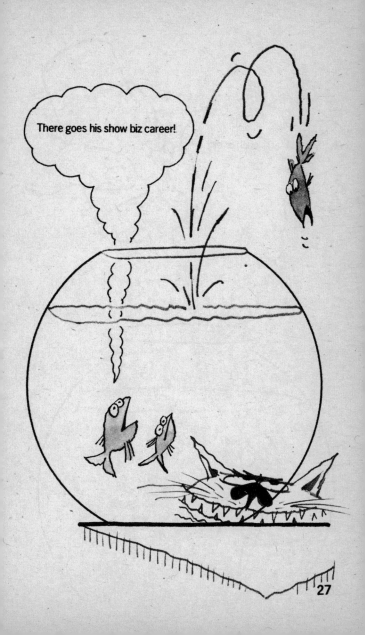

27

28

31

32

33

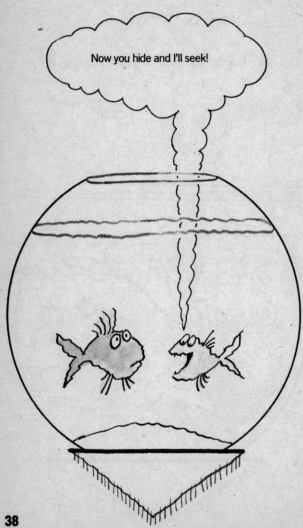

Many lobsters who started out as abominable pets have gone on to bigger and better things. Perhaps you've seen them on TV in ...

CLASSIC LATE SHOW LOBSTERS

42

LOBSTER KONG

LOBSTZILLER

THE LOBSTER OF OZ

KUNG FU LOBSTER

RAIDERS OF THE LOST LOBSTERS

51

DIRTY LOBSTER

53

CONAN THE LOBSTER

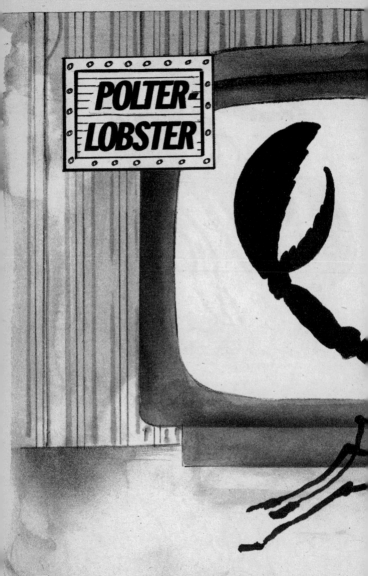

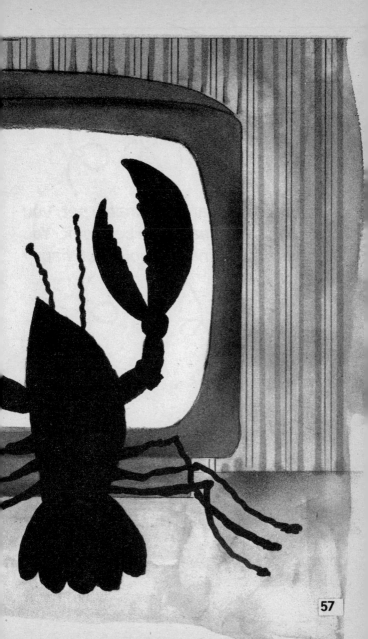

If you do have an abominable pet, you might as well make the best of it. You can start by making your pet happy with some ...

THOUGHTFUL GIFTS FOR YOUR FAVORITE ABOMINABLE PET

FOR YOUR PET LIZARD ...

A Well Seasoned Roll Of Flypaper

FOR YOUR PET FLEA CIRCUS...

An Unwashed Dog In Heat

FOR YOUR PET PRAIRIE DOG...

A Piece Of Wyoming

FOR YOUR PET TWIN SNAPPING TURTLES ...

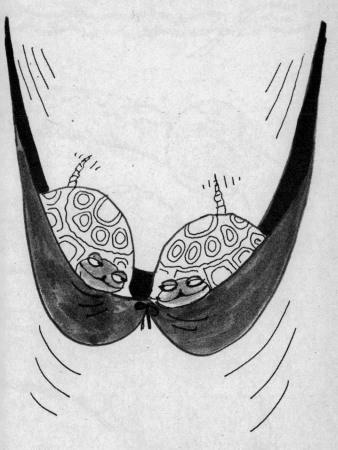

A Training Bra Love Seat Swing

FOR YOUR PET BOA CONSTRICTOR ...

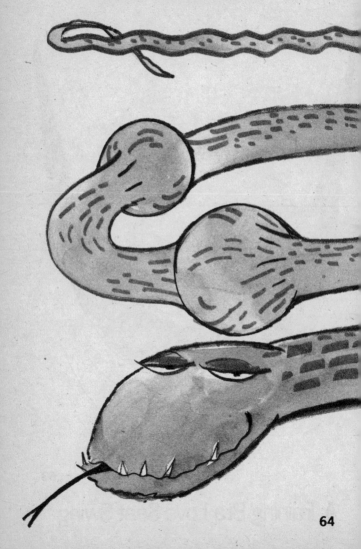

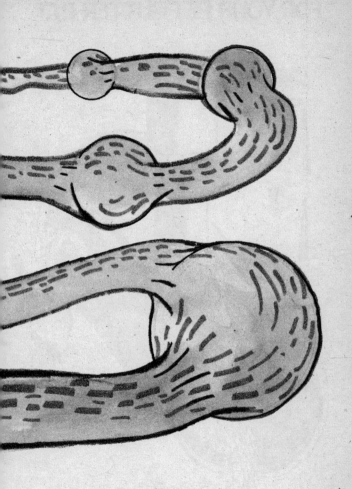

A Six Course Meal

FOR YOUR PET GUTTER RAT...

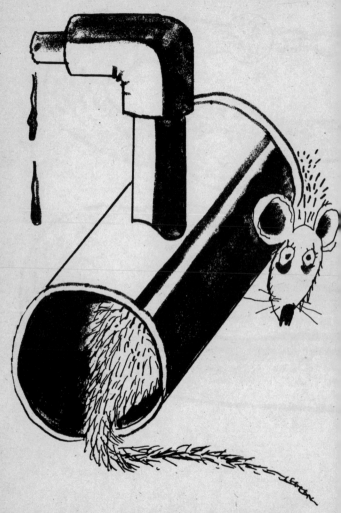

A Section Of Old Sewer Pipe

FOR YOUR PET TOAD ...

An Inflatable Princess Doll
With Pre-Puckered Lips

FOR YOUR PET THREE-TOED SLOTH ...

A Face-To-Face
Rendition Of Happy Birthday

FOR YOUR PET TSE-TSE FLY...

Three Free Meals

FOR YOUR PET SLUG ...

A Well-Oiled Access Ramp

FOR YOUR PET AARDVARK...

A Three-Day Weekend
On An Ant Farm

FOR YOUR PET SCORPION ...

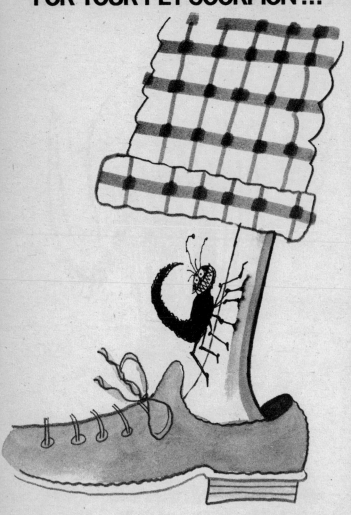

A Fake Pants Leg To Crawl Up

FOR YOUR PET BLACK WIDOW SPIDER ...

Balloon Supports For
A Web In A High Insect
Traffic Area

FOR YOUR PET BABY PIRANHA...

A Human Finger
Teething Ring

Some abominable creatures are, let's face it, pests! Until recently, only the swift strike from a king-size swatter brought minimum relief. Thanks to modern technology, we now have the aerosol can with its spray of instant equalizer. The question is: Is the aerosol spray, like the swatter, already doomed to obsolescence? Let's see what happens...

AFTER THE CLOUD LIFTS

THE FLY

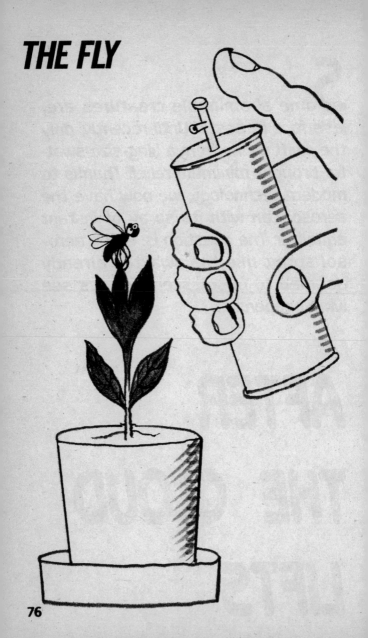

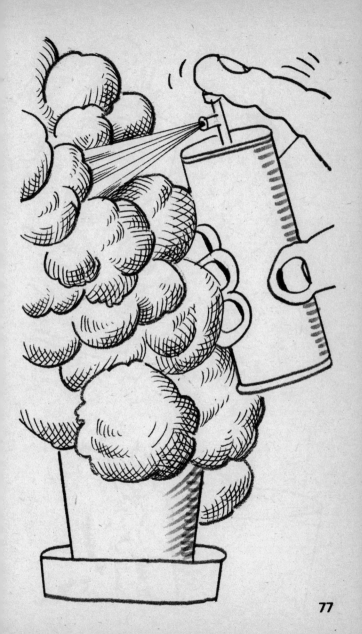

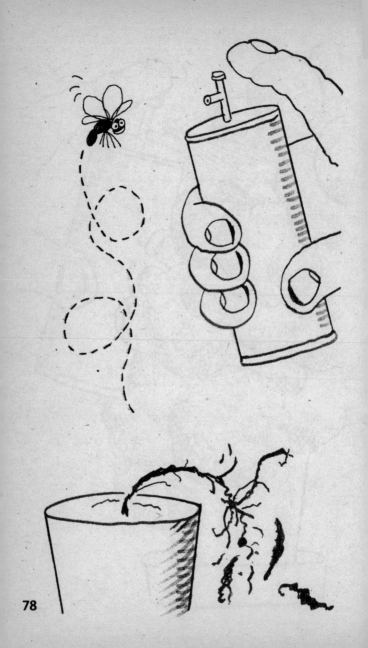

THE TERMITE

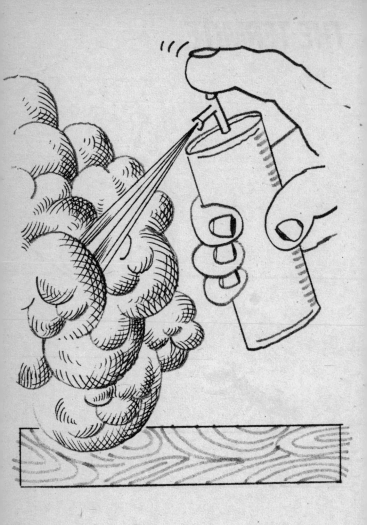

THE FLEA

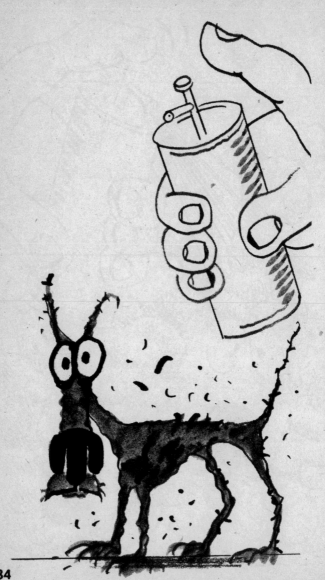

THE ROACH

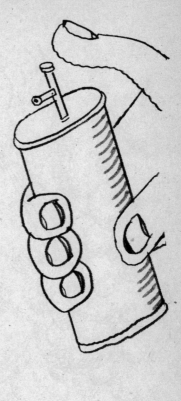

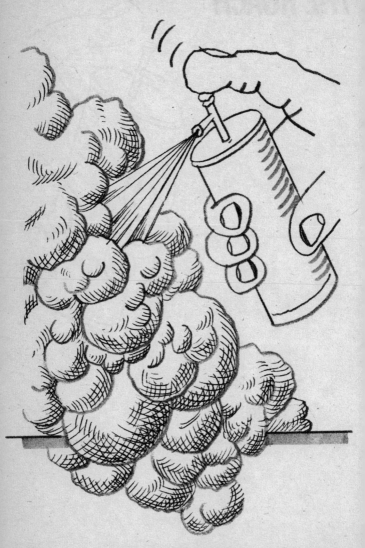

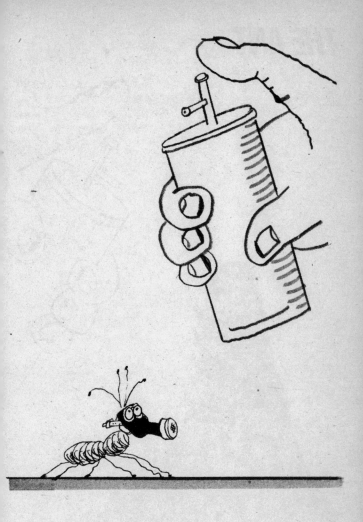

THE ANT

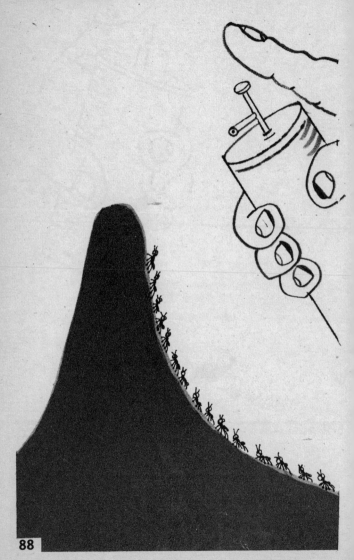

THE MOSQUITO

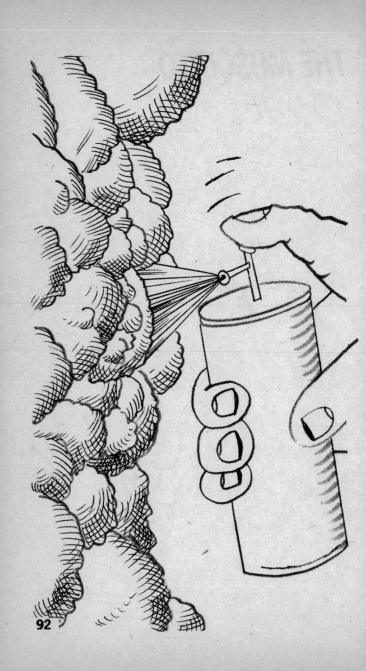

THE SPIDER

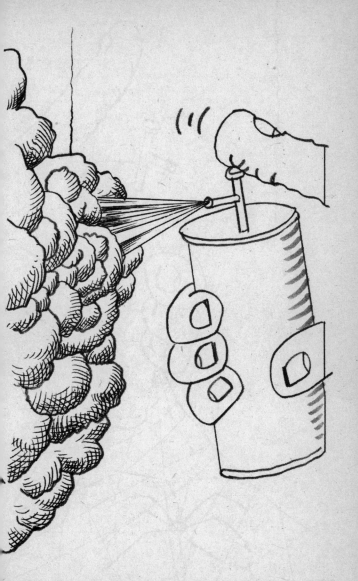

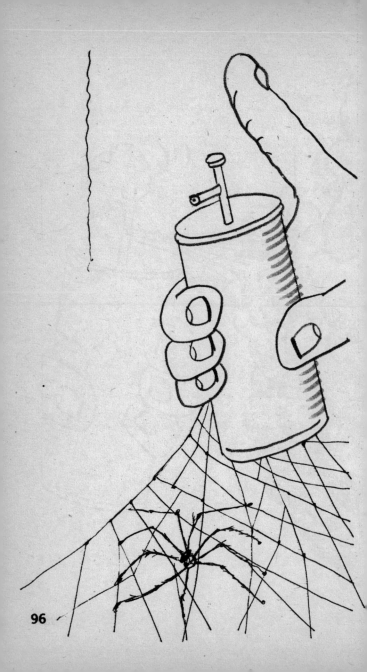

*T*urtles are one of the oldest creatures on earth. They have existed
since prehistoric times. And even way
back then, turtles were abominable
pets! They were slow and boring! But
prehistoric man, in his primitive wis-
dom, was able to use the turtle to his
advantage. Archeologists are just now
uncovering some of the many ...

PREHISTORIC

USES OF

TURTLES

PREHISTORIC TURTLE SKATEBOARD

PREHISTORIC TURTLE ARMY OUTFIT

enlisted man

officer

PREHISTORIC TURTLE
GAME BOARD

PREHISTORIC TURTLE WHEEL HUBCAP

PREHISTORIC TURTLE HARD HAT

PREHISTORIC TURTLE CREEK FORDER

PREHISTORIC TURTLE JUNK JEWELRY

As man progressed through the ages, he learned how to speak. And in time man also learned that turtles would sometimes respond to specific words. Armed with this information, man began to use speech to teach his abominable pet turtle simple tricks. If you are unfortunate enough to have an abominable pet turtle, you too can try to teach it some simple tricks using...

VOICE

COMMANDS

FOR OBEDIENT

TURTLES

DANCE!

BREAKDANCE!

SIT!

DO PUSH-UPS!

CATCH

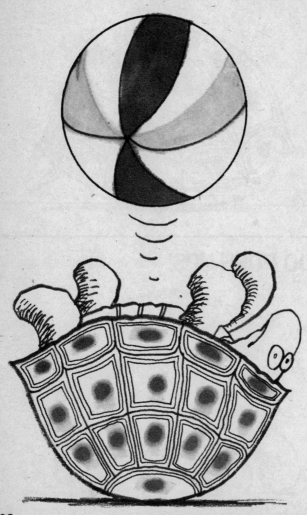

GET ME A COLD DRINK

EAT YOUR VEGGIES

*U*nfortunately, not all turtles are intelligent enough to obey voice commands. If you are stuck with a stupid turtle, you must revert back to prehistoric times and use the turtle to your advantage as best as possible. Here are some suggestions for ...

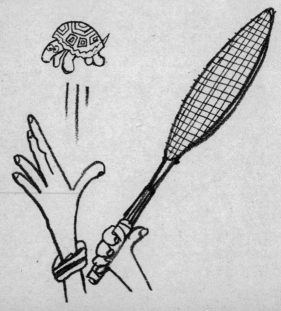

PRACTICAL MODERN DAY USES FOR PET TURTLES

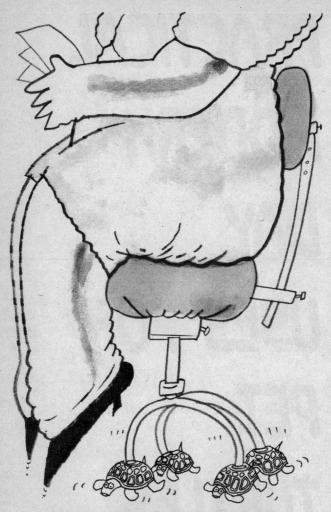

PET TURTLE CHAIR
ROLLERS

PET TURTLE MOBILE
BACK SCRUBBER

PET TURTLE READING
LIGHT SHADE

PET TURTLE COIN TRAY

PET TURTLE GYM EXERCISER

PET TURTLE ROULETTE
GAME MARKER

119

PET TURTLE TRUMPET MUTE

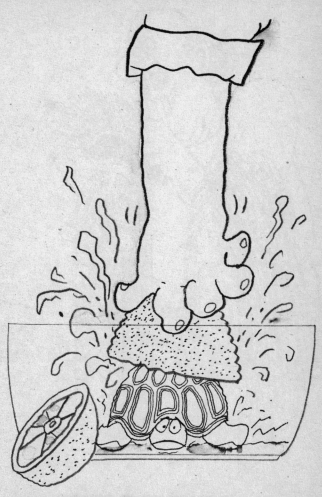

PET TURTLE GRAPEFRUIT JUICER

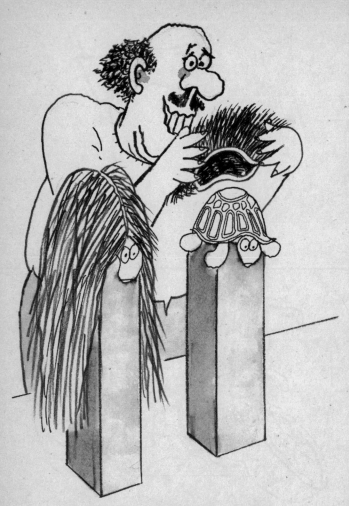

PET TURTLE WIG
SHAPER

PET TURTLE FLOATING
SOAP DISH

PET TURTLE TWIN MILITARY BRUSHES

PET TURTLE CYCLIST
CRASH HELMET

PET TURTLE PAPERWEIGHT

*B*esides the turtle, there have been many other examples of abominable creatures through the ages. Some of these creatures have been pets of some pretty famous people. Witness...

ABOMINABLE

PETS

OF

LEGENDS

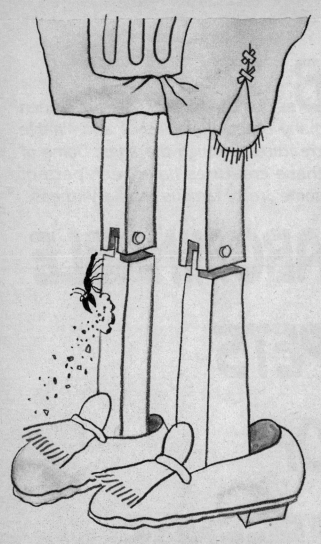

PINOCHIO'S PET TERMITE,
"WOODY"

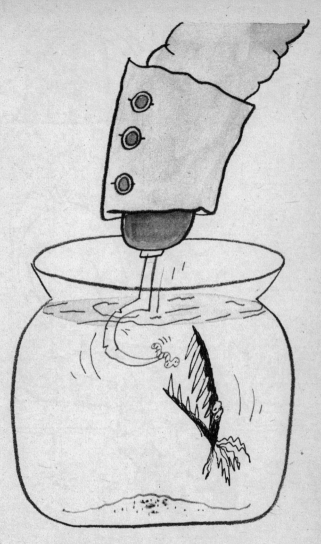

CAPTAIN HOOK'S PET
PIRANHA, *"SNAPPER"*

QUASIMODO'S PET WARTHOG,
"UGLY"

INDIANA JONES' PET BOA,
"WHIPPER"

HANSEL AND GRETEL'S CRUMB
EATING PET, *"BIRDIE"*

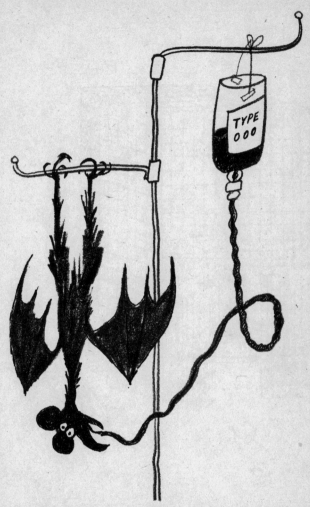

COUNT DRACULA'S PET BAT,
"HEMO"

HOUDINI'S PET GERBIL,
"SWIFTY"

CAPTAIN AHAB'S PET ALBINO
GOLDFISH, *"TOBY"*

135

THE PIED PIPER'S PET LEAD
RAT, *"LOLA"*

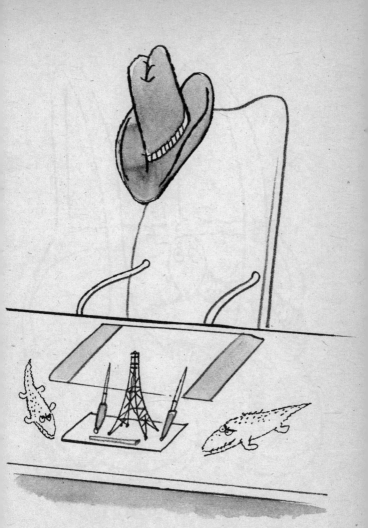

J.R. EWING'S PET TWIN GILA
MONSTERS *"MEAN"* AND
"EVIL"

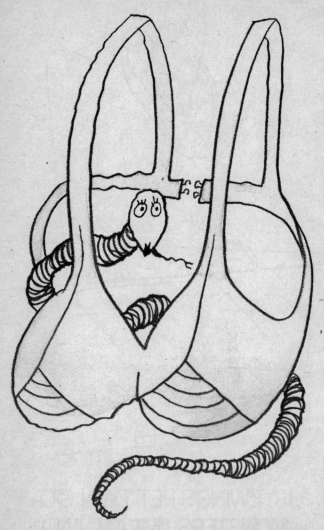

CLEOPATRA'S PET ASP, *"FALSY"*

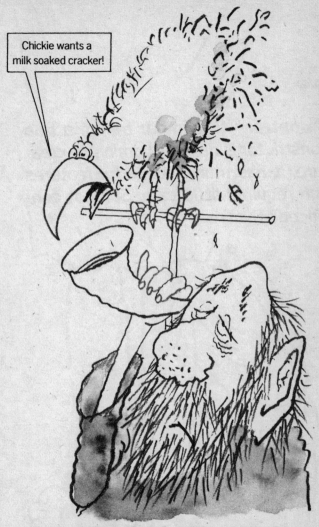

METHUSELAH'S 112-YEAR-OLD
PET PARROT, *"CHICKIE"* 139

Contrary to popular belief, a boa constrictor is not an abominable creature. It has many wonderful features and requires little care. Still not convinced? Then read on ...

FOR

BOA

CONSTRICTOR

LOVERS

ONLY

BOA CONSTRICTORS CAN BE
AFFECTIONATE...

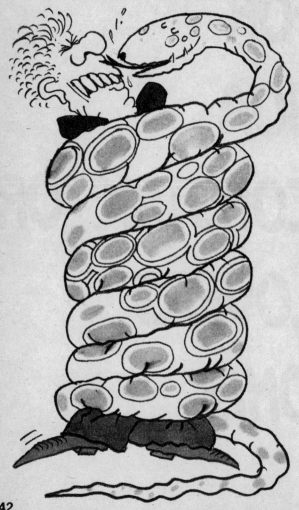

PLAYFUL...

OR *USEFUL.*

THEY CAN *FEED* THEMSELVES ...

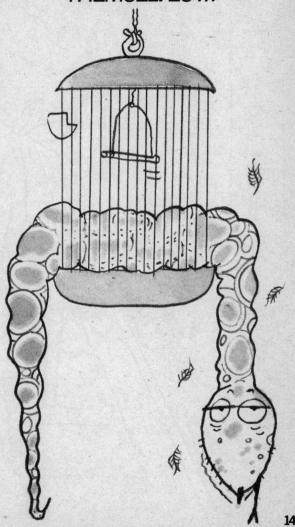

ARE *GOOD AT SPORTS…*

BOA CONSTRICTORS ARE
GREAT WITH TODDLERS...

CAN *ADMINISTER THE HEIMLICH MANEUVER TO CHOKING VICTIMS ...*

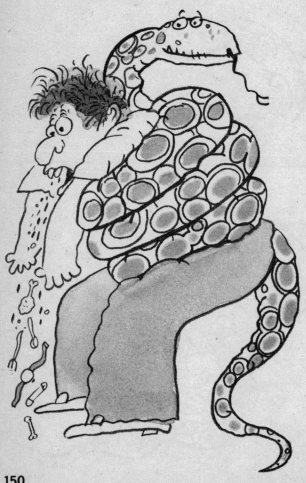

AND ARE *HELPFUL WITH THE BEDRIDDEN.*

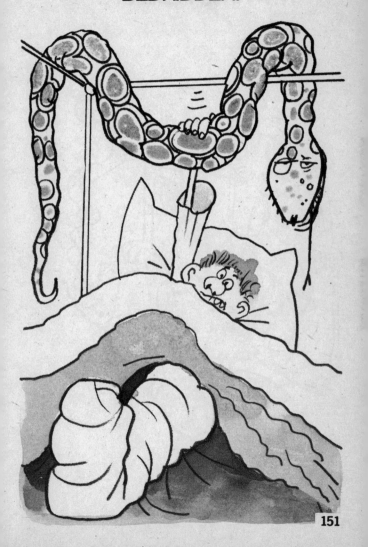

THEY ARE ALSO *WONDERFUL WITH THE ELDERLY...*

HELPFUL WITH THE HOUSEWORK...

AND *MAKE GREAT* EMERGENCY INFANT SEATS.

BOA CONSTRICTORS CAN ALSO *ACT AS A CHAPERON* ...

MAKE YOU LOOK SLIMMER ...

AND EVEN *SAVE LIVES!*

BEST OF ALL, BOA CONSTRICTORS ARE *EASILY STORED!*

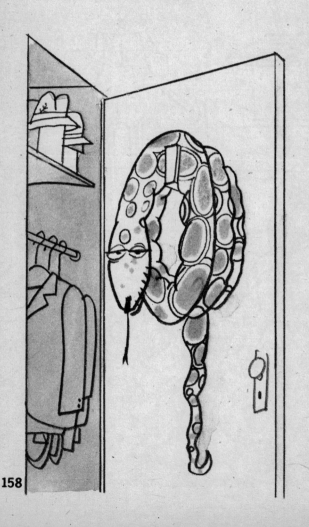

The absolute worst thing that can happen is to encounter an abominable creature owned by someone who doesn't realize it's an abominable creature. These people are obnoxious! They seem to think that by making a little remark or joke, everyone will automatically excuse the abominable behavior of their abominable pet. Surely, at one time or another, you've heard all of these ...

ABOMINABLE CREATURE CLICHÉS

160

161

162

163

166

169

171

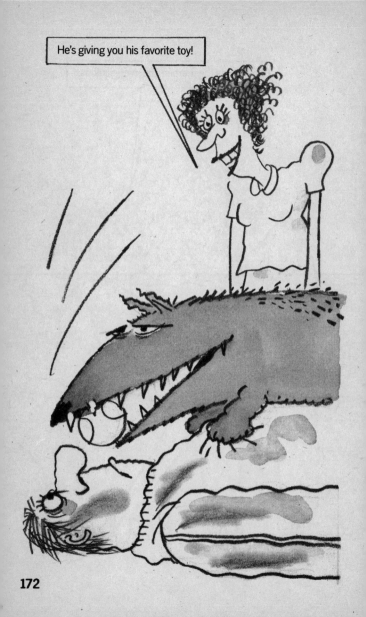

173

LOBSTERS

TO

THE

RESCUE

LOBSTER FAT MAN'S
SHOE HORN

LOBSTER EMERGENCY JACK

LOBSTER SENIOR CITIZEN COMPANION

LOBSTER MOUSE
EXTERMINATOR

LOBSTER LIVE WIRE TESTER

LOBSTER PLUMBER'S HELPER

LOBSTER TV REMOTE
CONTROL

LOBSTER LADDER LATCH

184 LOBSTER INVALID WALKER

PARTING

SHOTS

LOBSTER RADIATOR CAP REMOVER

LOBSTER BOMB DISARMER 187

**LOBSTER FIRST-AID
TOURNIQUET**

**LOBSTER VAMPIRE
PROTECTOR**